The World According to Ed

a poetry collection by

Ed Lawrence Hagape

Ed L Hagape

2017

Thanks for being
a inspiration and
mentor to me
~ Ed Lawrence
Eduarte Hagape

The World According to Ed
by Ed Lawrence Hagape

Editor:
Rich Hill

Contributor & Front and Back Cover:
John Ellsworth

ISBN: 978-1-387-03546-5

The World According to Ed
by Ed Lawrence Hagape

This poetry collection is dedicated to my family, long-time residents of the South of Market neighborhood of San Francisco, Filipinos everywhere, De Marillac Academy, and the hustlers who try to do anything for the people they love.

The World According to Ed
by Ed Lawrence Hagape

Contents

The World According to Ed
by Ed Lawrence Hagape

Foreword

Ed Lawrence Hagape

What you are about to read was once just ordinary poetry homework assignments. Words put to paper for a grade, not knowing that they would become a bigger message. One summer evening when I was on my iPad, my fingers then lead me to my old poetry file from middle school. I started to reread the old poems and I relived the feelings I had when writing them. I also saw a bigger picture come to life when rereading these words.

I saw a vision of people understanding where the other person comes from. This was the seed that made this anthology a reality. Where we come from, where we live, our experiences there: these are all shared as people. We can easily forget that while we all have different experiences, we should sometimes listen to the other point of view to understand.

I invite you to read about my experiences and connect these words to your own experiences. Not only can we see the world through our own eyes, but we can gain a new lens and see *The World According to Ed.*

Immigration

 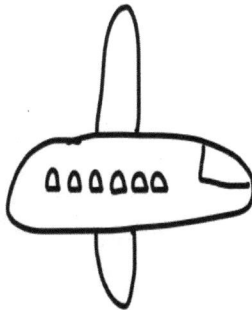 

I Live in the Doorway Between

I live in the doorway between the
Philippines and America.
Two distant lands divided
by one vast ocean.
Two different cultures that
I have to go meet.

Philippines: 7,107 islands of land.
Where there are shops and
street vendors everywhere.
Tricycles and jeepneys
for transportation.
It feels like a sauna.
Everyone always wants a
better opportunity.

America: Land all united.
I look up at the buildings touching the sky.
I look with awe as the city twinkles in the moonlight.
More cars line every street.
At first, this land felt weird,
but I got used to it.

Just cross the ocean to open both doors.
But it's easier said than done.
I live in the doorway between the
Philippines and America.

Going East

There's a better opportunity
just across the Pacific.

A place called America,
that's where we shall be.

Working tirelessly to get
visas and passports
at the U.S. Embassy.

And when I'm accepted,
I'm ready to leave.

Get ready to pack
and head on a U.S. bound plane;
better opportunities are
just 15 hours away.

I land at an airport called SFO,
for this is the gateway
to my new home.

I look with awe at the
new places I see.

I see the city twinkle
in the moonlight.

The World According to Ed
by Ed Lawrence Hagape

And as I look all around me
I don't know where to go,
but I just know,
this is my new home.

This Foreign Land

I remember when I came to America.
Heading to a Philippine Airlines plane,
going to this foreign land.
Coming to this
land of opportunity.
Coming to this
land to start a new life.

Landing at SFO,
my dad was waiting by the terminal.
I hopped in a car and sat on a
"fancy" seat, which I now know is a car seat.
My dad was strapping on an item called
a seat belt, which I had never heard of before.
Heading down the highway,
I had never seen all this stuff before.
Highway 101, Bay Bridge, and Daly City
read several signs.
When I hopped out off the car, I saw
a foreign street twinkling in the night.

Coming to a home I had never seen before.
The only thing that was familiar to me was
the toys my dad had bought.
In this foreign land,
I still sang the Philippine anthem.
In this foreign land
that I now call home.

In or Not

Dedicated to the immigrants who came through Angel Island.

You prepare for
long hours to go to
this new land.

You hope to make a new living.

You hop on a boat and
wait for long months.

You head to his new land;
for many, they start at
Angel Island.

You hop off the boat,
leave all your luggage,
and head to this big building.

There you are separated.
Chinese here, others there;
Women and children here, men there.

You are interrogated for long hours;
asked stupid questions to see you are
who you say you are.

The World According to Ed
by Ed Lawrence Hagape

If you're fake, you go back to your
home country.

People wait in detention barracks
waiting to enter.

While others like the wealthy
are allowed to enter,
you wait more long months
trying to be legal.

Many are sent back,
but you are accepted.

You pack all your stuff and
get all your papers.

Welcome to America,
I know you can do it.

San Francisco

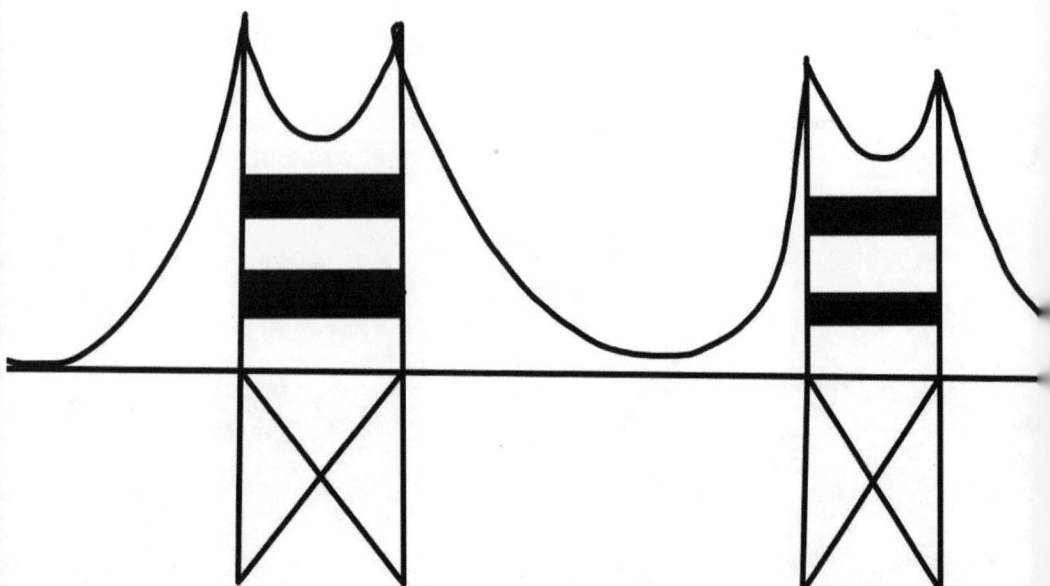

A Changing Area

Before I was able to see the sky and the sun.
Now there is a high rise blocking the view.

Before that plot of land was a parking lot.
Now there is a housing development but it doesn't house
the low income.

Before the low income were able to afford rent prices.
Now those prices are through the roof.

Before a family used to live here and an old lady there.
Now a person with more money than the family and the old
lady lives there.

Before a long time business used to be here.
Now there is a cafe selling $10 coffee.

Before Muni buses used to be a driver's nuisance.
Now it's corporate buses and rideshare cars that irritate
drivers.

Before there was a mayor who listened to long-time
residents.
Now we have a mayor putting money before people.

Before we fought to make our streets safer.
Now on top of that, we fight to preserve these streets.

SoMa

My neighborhood is
SoMa.

It is in the middle
of everything.

A couple of steps and you are
in the dark side of SF with
crime and drugs.

A couple of steps and you are
in Downtown SF, where
most people want to go.

Cars, buses, and trucks
pass by every day.

You can hear horns, street performers
and people hanging out.

But, you can also hear sirens,
people selling drugs, and
people yelling or talking to themselves.

Tourists come to
have a vacation,
While locals scramble to
get from point A to point B.

The World According to Ed
by Ed Lawrence Hagape

It is like the New York
of the West.

Skyscrapers are
everywhere.

The buildings cast a shadow
on the whole neighborhood.

There is no place
I'd rather be.

SoMa is my neighborhood;
SoMa is my home.

Bay Bridge

Two bridges connected by
one island.

In the west, the gray stately towers.
In the east, one majestic tower.

During rush hour it looks
more like a parking lot than a bridge.

People with things to do and places to go just wait.
Some frustrated, some jamming to the radio
to pass the time.

Below the bridge is the beautiful
blue waters of the bay.

Humongous shipping boats go underneath
the bridge as they finish their long
journey across the Pacific.

In the night time, streams of light
twinkle on its cables making
an incredible light show.

The Bay Bridge,
underrated but glorious.

Golden Gate Bridge

Towering high between
SF and Marin County.

The misty fog
rolls by.

The color is international orange,
don't call it red.

Cars roll by it
everyday.

People also walk and
bike on it.
The two towers
are above your head.

The city skyline on one side,
the Pacific Ocean on the other.

Underneath is the
raging waters of the bay.

You stop and take a picture
of the bridge and the views.

Then you want to visit it again.

A Perfect Scene

Imagine this.

It is the holiday mood
on Market Street.

The snowflakes are
hung at each light pole.

It is also raining.

The puddles make a cool
color effect on the street.

People, cars, buses, and trucks
pass by.

That's my perfect scene.

My Dream Day

What a sunny day!

The birds are chirping,
the kids are playing.

The sky is blue and there are
no clouds at all.

I walk out of my house
and breathe the fresh air.

I wander through
Downtown SF.

There's no homework,
there's no stress.

It's just me relaxing.

What a day that can be!

For a Better World

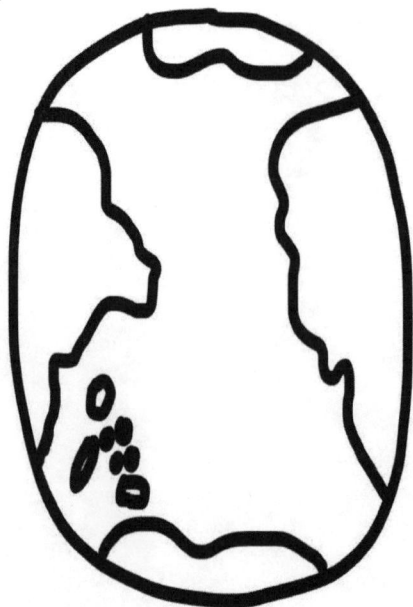

The World According to Ed

The World According to Ed would be one of peace.
Where weapons are dropped and hands are raised up high.
Where all people are able to come together.
Where people are not afraid to be with each other.

The World According to Ed would be one of joy.
Where people smile and wave to each other.
Where people's worries and struggles are now diminished.
Where a candle is relit when it has been blown out.

The World According to Ed would be one of love.
Where people love each other no matter the labels.
Where we turn an eye for an eye to love thy neighbor.
Where unconditional love prevails.

The World According to Ed would be one of great
well-being.

From None to Tons

It can be that person
on the corner.
It can be that person
in a poor village.
It can be that person
living in a bad neighborhood.

They can still have opportunities.
Opportunities that they may
have thought they couldn't get.
Someday they'll be working and
living a good life.
You'll be surprised.

What's Really Your Message?

Riots and police everywhere.
People looting stores.
Tear gas, smoke, and broken glass
line the street.
Chaos throughout a city.

A city on lockdown, a city on a
state of emergency.

What's really your message?
Justice or abusing someone's name.
Using a tragic loss to wreck a whole city.
Go and show your freedom of speech.
Don't go overboard and wreck stuff.

Go and show your anger peacefully.
If you riot and loot,
your fellow neighbors are affected.
Local businesses are hurt.
The local economy is threatened.
Children can't go to school.
Parents losing money since
they can't go to work.
Everyone is hurt.

What's really your message?

World Peace

World peace is,
Nonviolence.

World peace is,
Equality.

World peace is,
Love.

World peace is,
Understanding.

World peace means,
No Wars.

World peace means,
No Injustice.

World peace means,
No Fighting.

World peace means,
All People Are Equal.

The Unlikely Weapon

A pen is an
unlikely weapon.

Use it and it can
change people.

It can change a
society.

One signature and countries
can be at war.

One signature and countries
can be at peace.

A pen is an extension
of your mind.

Use it wisely.

Worship

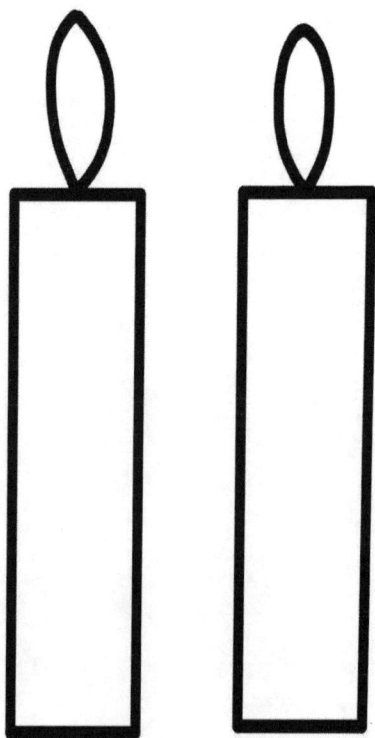

Temple of God

I am a temple of God.
He dwells in me through the Spirit.

Right inside my soul,
He makes His home.

He walks with me.
He celebrates with me.
He cries with me.

In this earthly pilgrimage,
He is guiding me.

He is with me
wherever I go.

He dwells in you also.
For it is said He dwells among all of us.
He shall be our God and we shall be His people.

My Soul

My soul is the sound of
the wind blowing through
a field of grass.

My soul is the color of
the snow high above a
mountain top.

My soul is
one of a kind;
it will never be copied.

My soul is a fire,
ready to enlighten the
whole world.

My soul is the image of
an eagle flying high
and free.

My soul is a creation
of God.

Sacred Meal

We gather on this holy day of Sabbath.
Gathered around this holy table.
On this table, we offer up the lamb, the final lamb.

We honor He who died with bread and wine.
With his holy hands, the priest turns the bread and wine
To His body and blood.

We break this bread and drink the wine,
All gathered around this holy table
For the most sacred meal.

Cross

A cross has different
meanings. It can mean
you need medical help.
It can mean what Jesus
died for. It can be a T but
lowercased. People wear it to show their faith.
You can see them high above a church. It can be
seen from miles. It can be known right away. The
cross is used to show the
Christian faith. It can be
seen on an altar. It can be
seen at people's houses. It is
seen in many rosaries. It is seen
in many accessories. It is a very
powerful symbol. That is a cross.

Motivation

Happiness :)

Happiness is
waking up on a weekend.

Happiness is
smiling at everyone you meet.

Happiness is
joy.

Happiness is
sunshine and rainbows.

Happiness is
peace.

Happiness is
celebrating each moment
of your life.

Happiness is
family and friends.

Happiness does not
come from possessions.

Freedom

Freedom is
doing what you want to do.

Freedom is
saying what you want to say.

Freedom is
believing in anything you want.

Freedom is
making your own choices.

Freedom is
going down the path you want to go to.

Life

Life is great.
Life is tough.
Life is challenging.
Life is a mystery.

You don't know what lies ahead.
You don't know what happens next.
You don't know which path to take.
You don't know what choices to make.

Just go!
Make the most of it.
If you have an obstacle, conquer it.
Remember, the sky's the limit!

A New Day

Arise from your sleep.
Get up and start fresh.

Eat breakfast,
brush your teeth,
take a shower,
get dressed.

Walk out of your house
with confidence.

Go make new memories.
Go seize the day.

A New Day is here!

Rocketship

10,
9, 8...
Heading
into your
rocketship.

7,6,5...
Sit and buckle up.

4,3,2,1...
BLASTOFF!

You are ready for
a new adventure.

An adventure to new
places.

You'll meet new people,
you'll see new sights.

Just remember,
enjoy the ride!

Light

Light gives you sight.
Light is the thing that
illuminates any place.
Light gives you energy.
We all need light.

Walking

Step-by-step on a journey.
You don't know where you're going.
Just let your legs and the wind take you places.

Music

Go to a radio station
and "pump up the jam".

You know some of the songs.

Others you may not know.

Then, your song
pops up.

You start to dance to the beat
or sing along to the song.

It doesn't matter if you're
at work, school, or even on the bus.

You will get your
boogie on!

About the Author

Ed Lawrence Hagape

Originally from the Philippines, Ed Lawrence Hagape now calls San Francisco, CA home. Ed is currently in high school and looks forward to graduation in 2020. He strives for excellence and loves to amuse people he meets with his accent and personality; Ed knows how to light up a room and can surely make you smile. Each day he tries to find ways to improve in all aspects of his life. Ed aspires to complete college, start a successful career and live a full and happy life.

Ed's writing has been featured in *Born Within* from De Marillac Academy and *Five Quarts of Kindness* from 826 Valencia. He also jumped at the chance to interview Buster Posey, catcher for the San Francisco Giants. His interview can be found in the April 2016 issue of *Giants* magazine.

Twitter: @ehagape
Instagram: @edhagape